Meditations for Financial Freedom

DeForest B. Soaries, Jr.

DBS Solutions, LLC

Published by DBS Solutions, LLC

Copyright © 2023 DeForest B. Soaries, Jr. All rights reserved.

Book Packaging: Earl Cox & Associates Worldwide https://earlcox.com
Cover design by Benny Goodman

ISBN 13: 978-1-7356124-3-0
LCNN: 2016933840

Cataloging in Publication Data

Names:	Soaries, DeForest B., author.
Title:	Meditations for financial freedom; V.4 / DeForest B. Soaries, Jr.
Description:	First edition.	Monmouth Junction, NJ : DBS Solutions, LLC, [2023]	Series: Meditations for financial freedom ; Vol 4
Identifiers:	ISBN: 978-1-7356124-3-0	978-1-7356124-2-3 (ebook)
Subjects:	LCSH: Finance, Personal--Religious aspects--Christianity.	Saving and investment--Religious aspects--Christianity.	Retirement--Planning--Religious aspects--Christianity.	Entrepreneurship--Religious aspects--Christianity.	Consumer credit--Religious aspects--Christianity.	BISAC: RELIGION / Biblical Meditations / General.	RELIGION / Biblical Criticism & Interpretation / General.	BUSINESS & ECONOMICS / Personal Finance / General.
Classification:	LCC: HG179 .S63 2016	DDC: 332.024--dc23

Printed in the United States of America

First Edition: 2023

TABLE OF CONTENTS

INTRODUCTION

There are many ways to study the Bible. Many people find the stories in the Bible the most accessible way to connect with scripture and to find relevance in the Word of God. The power of a story is that one can connect his or her own story to what they are reading. This volume of Meditations for Financial Freedom attempts to do just that – connect the stories of 1 and 2 Kings to other stories that can add value to the reader's financial journey.

These books of the Bible describe a period of Israel's history when the work of prophets Elijah and his successor, Elisha, was prominent. These men continuously spoke truth to power in ways that inspire prophets today. Of course, the concept of prophesy and prophetic utterance has been somewhat distorted by those who seek to turn prophesying into profiteering and turn religion into a business that enriches leaders, rather than a movement that liberates followers.

Elijah and Elisha demonstrate the kind of prophecy that appropriately declares the will of God in response to the social, economic, and spiritual conditions facing God's people. It is in that sense that I offer this book as a prophetic writing. It is not my intent to offer formulas for success or religious quick fixes to financial challenges. Instead, I offer practical examples of Biblical principles derived from Bible stories with relevance and influence in life today. And I believe there are some urgent messages that should be taken seriously.

The kind of faith as described in *Day 13* of this book is very important for people to understand. Our understanding of faith has become so diluted in the modern age that real faith, as displayed by the poor widow, has become almost incomprehensible.

The practical need for having a living will and healthcare directive is imperative as medical technology advances, and we find ourselves moving from place to place more than ever. *Day 23* takes advantage of God's instructions to King Hezekiah to promote the completion of living wills. I have heard this text preached and taught all my life and never heard anyone attach it to this most pressing need.

Finally, efforts to achieve financial freedom cannot ignore the need to advocate for economic justice as described in *Day 25*. While personal choices have much to do with individual financial outcomes, systemic issues and how many institutions exert power cannot be ignored.

I pray that you will be blessed by these devotional meditations. I also pray that you will have an even greater love for the Bible as you appreciate its ability to motivate and inform your financial journey.

God bless you and yours.

DeForest B. Soaries, Jr.

1 OLD AGE

Verse

"When King David was very old, he could not keep warm even when they put covers over him."
1 Kings 1:1

Thought

When former President George Herbert Walker Bush died in 2019 at the age of 94, he had been planning to skydive on his 95th birthday the following year. He had established a post-retirement tradition of parachuting from a plane on every fifth birthday, starting when he turned 75 years old. By his 90th birthday, although his health had declined and he was confined to a wheelchair, Mr. Bush still dove from an airplane in a tandem skydive. He never let his age or his physical condition rob him of his life.

David had been king of Israel for 40 years and the time had come when he was so advanced in age that his weak and frail body could not retain its natural heat. Neither a blanket nor a young maiden, who had been assigned to him, could warm or arouse him. Verse 4 of this chapter says, *"The woman was very beautiful; she took care of the king and waited on him, but the king had no sexual relations with her."* This was not the David of old!

Every season of our lives finds us incapable of doing certain things that were previously easily to do. One need not to be nearing death to appreciate the reality that our lives go through stages that result in undeniable and irreversible changes. The important challenge represented by this fact is that we must be aware of and engaged in our abilities while we have them, and we must also prepare for when that season comes to an end.

Mr. Bush was too old and too weak to do the tasks he had done when he was a younger man. Had he attempted to dive from a plane alone on his 90th birthday, the outcome would likely have been disastrous. His acceptance of a "jump partner" to whom he was strapped made that activity possible and successful. Likewise, had David attempted to confront an enemy like Goliath at the latter stage of his life, he would have been easily defeated. Both of these men remind us that there is, in fact, a season for everything. (Ecclesiastes 3).

They also remind us that until we breathe our last breath, there are important things we can do. Mr. Bush accomplished a skydive four years before he died. David accomplished giving a charge to his son and naming him king before his death. Both men were weak, but both men functioned using the strength that they had.

We are all going to age. The better we use the time that we have now, the more gracefully we will embrace the transitions that our lives will experience.

Prayer

God, help me to age productively and gracefully. Amen.

Decision

Today I have decided to: _____

_____

_____

_____

_____

ULTIMATE ENDING

Verse

"Then David rested with his ancestors and was buried in the City of David." 1 Kings 2:10 NIV

Thought

Efforts to stay alive are core to the human personality. We do an unlimited number of tasks to prolong our lives and to maintain quality of life during our lives. Despite the fact that death is the only certainty in life, we passionately avoid thinking about and planning for death.

We often use language to avoid using the word death. We prefer euphemisms such as pass away and kick the bucket, among others. When we are forced to say anything about our inevitable demise, many of us will say "if anything ever happens to me" as if there is a possibility that we may be exempted from the "anything" of death.

David had a spectacular life and an amazing tenure as king. But he died. Unfortunately, we live much better lives when we remain aware of the fact that we are only here to pass through. That is not to suggest that we should be preoccupied with or persistently distracted by death. What it means is that we should prepare for the inevitable transition.

The last chapter of my book, *Say Yes When Life Says No, is The No of an Ultimate Ending*. In that chapter, I described my family's pain when my father died at only 47 years of age. Dad's death left me as head of our family and responsible for handling all of our family affairs. That was almost a bad joke since I was barely handling my personal affairs. However, this is how I described my responsibility: "Although it was difficult emotionally, handling my dad's affairs was a piece of cake because he had everything so well organized." (Pg. 201)

To be organized and to minimize the complications caused by our transition from this world, we should at least have a:

- List of all assets and liabilities
- Last will and testament
- Living will and health care directive
- Life insurance with updated list of beneficiaries
- Place where legal documents are kept
- Preferences or plans for funeral arrangements

David almost failed to identify his wishes for leadership in the kingdom after his demise. This resulted in things getting out of control between his sons. Fortunately, he was forewarned and heeded this warning by naming Solomon as his successor.

We owe it to our respective "kingdoms" – no matter how small – to be prepared for our ultimate ending.

Prayer

God, teach me to number my days. Amen.

Decision

Today I have decided to: _____

_____

_____

_____

_____

BENEVOLENT GRACE

Verse

Then the king sent for Shimei and said to him, "Build yourself a house in Jerusalem and live there, but do not go anywhere else. The day you leave and cross the Kidron Valley, you can be sure you will die; your blood will be on your own head." 1 Kings 2:36 & 37 NIV

Then the king gave the order to Benaiah son of Jehoiada, and he went out and struck Shimei down and he died. The kingdom was now established in Solomon's hands. 1 Kings 2:46 NIV

Thought

Everyone possesses power. One of our most significant challenges is deciding what power we wield and then, how to use it. The word "power" causes us to think of rich and famous people – those with titles and in positions of authority. That is the kind of power that Solomon had. It may seem, from these verses, that King David ordered the execution of Shimei because he disobeyed his order not to leave Jerusalem. But Shimei was not sentenced to die because he left Jerusalem; he had previously disrespected and slandered King David. It was, however, King Solomon who ordered Shimei's execution, and this happened long after he had actually shown him grace and allowed him to live in Jerusalem. For abusing the gift of Solomon's grace, Shimei paid with his life.

It is not only God who grants us grace, but people also extend us grace and we must be careful not to take it for granted. Do you remember the old saying, *"give them an inch and they will take a yard"*? I learned that lesson when I inherited a four-family house from my paternal grandmother and had to drive to Brooklyn every month to collect rent from the tenants. One woman was consistently late with her rent, and it became very inconvenient for me to drive back and forth between New York and New Jersey several times a month to collect her rent.

I allowed my tenants to pay their rent a few days late without any late fees or penalties as most landlords do. And knowing that this woman usually needed more time, I decided to delay my rent collection visit until the 5th of the month instead of the 1st. When I arrived, the tenant greeted me warmly at her apartment and asked why I was there. She then told me boldly that she had had the rent money on the 1st of the month, but since I did not show up to collect and several days had passed, she no longer had the money to pay me.

What I thought was the kindness of extended grace turned into the abuse of grace. When we fail to acknowledge that grace, by definition, is not deserved, we tend to be ungrateful for grace. Needless to say, I no longer extended much grace to that tenant.

Both King David and his son, King Solomon, had the political right to kill Shimei simply because he was a descendant of their adversary, King Saul. But they were gracious and let him live. Solomon even let him live *in* Jerusalem. Shimei's plight should stir us to recognize and show gratitude in response to the grace that we receive. Or like him, our destruction will be on our own heads.

Prayer

God, help me to be more mindful of and grateful for the grace I receive. Amen

Decision

Today I have decided to: _____

_____

_____

_____

_____

SUPERIOR STRATEGY

Verse

"Solomon made an alliance with Pharaoh, king of Egypt, and married his daughter. He brought her to the City of David until he finished building his palace and the temple of the Lord, and the wall around Jerusalem." 1 Kings 3:1 NIV

Thought

When my sons played basketball in school and community competitions, I often told them that a team with inferior talent but superior strategy could win any competition. They learned this a few times, but the most memorable, I believe, was when they played in a three-on-three tournament against a team of very tall opponents who looked like giants compared to my boys' team. However, the shorter team adopted a tactic to shoot only three-point shots against their rivals who dominated rebounds and the advantage to shoot close to the basket. When my boys' team won the championship game, the taller team was totally confused as to how these little guys could beat them. The answer was simple; they adopted a superior strategy and it worked!

A winning plan requires knowing exactly what you want to accomplish – the goal. It requires a willingness to do something that has never been done before to yield results of great value. And it also requires identifying and securing resources you need to win.

Solomon knew what he wanted and he had a plan. He wanted peace and prosperity, and what better way to secure that than to form an alliance with the most powerful nation in the region at that time. Israel has always been a small nation. But with Egypt as an ally, Israel now had capacity it could not have on its own. By marrying Pharaoh's daughter, Solomon adopted strategy to secure the most reliable political connection he could obtain. Imagine the king of Israel marrying the daughter of the king of the nation that had previously enslaved his people for 400 years! I'm sure the old folks must have been quite upset about it. But Solomon had a plan.

Not everyone understands tactic. More importantly, not everyone understands the need for tact. Having a goal without strategy translates into having a *what* without a *how*. This is true for all aspects of our lives including our finances.

Many people have told me they don't have enough money to have a financial strategy. My response is that without a strategy, you will never have enough money!

Prayer

God, help develop and execute superior strategy.

Decision

Today I have decided to: _____

_____

_____

_____

_____

WISE HEART

Verse

"I will do what you have asked. I will give you a wise and discerning heart, so that there will never have been anyone like you, nor will there ever be." 1 Kings 3:12 NIV

Thought

My favorite stories as a child were tales and fables that involved people who possessed magical powers. I can't imagine any child being able to ignore such fiction. The popularity of "The Arabian Nights", featuring a young Aladdin, who discovers an oil lamp that has magical powers confirms my opinion. In addition to his magic ring that gives him certain magical powers, Aladdin's lamp produced a genie that helped him become very rich by accessing unlimited power. The genie, the magic and the conquests of Aladdin make this such an intriguing story that Disney created an animated movie that was seen by millions of admiring fans.

This idea of a supernatural genie who does the bidding of its owner bears an unfortunate resemblance to the view that many people have of God. The idea that God does the bidding of those that believe and have faith in God has become a mainstream theological perspective in the modern age.

There have always been people that used religion and religious practices for personal gain and political power. But not since Martin Luther opposed the use of money in the 16th century Catholic church has there been a greater need to oppose many of the current practices and teachings of the so-called Christian Prosperity Gospel. Led by very popular and influential clergy who skillfully use technology and media, this movement has turned God into a cosmic Santa Claus who rewards those with sufficient faith with the desires of their materialistic and prodigal hearts. They have turned God into a kind of genie that one's faith can rub out of a "lamp" and ask us to name and claim what we want.

Today's promoters of Christian prosperity seem to admire Aladdin more than they admire Solomon. Aladdin pursued the acquisition of money and power. He was even able to use his new found power source to undermine the wedding plans of a young princess that he desired and, ultimately, married.

In contrast, Solomon asked God to give him a *wise heart*. With a wise heart he could be discerning and use his power effectively; he could lead with integrity; he would be a good judge of character.

Knowledge is great, and there is nothing wrong with attaining wealth as Solomon did. But we require wisdom to understand what to do with our knowledge. Knowledge shows us how to become wealthy, while wisdom shows us how to handle the wealth we have attained.

Wisdom will sustain personal success and nurture the character that God desires in us. Wisdom, however, is not attained through magic. Wisdom comes from a God who is the maker of wisdom.

Prayer

God, give me wisdom. Amen.

Decision

Today I have decided to: _____

_____

_____

_____

_____

COMMUNITY SAFETY

Verse

"During Solomon's lifetime, Judah and Israel, from Dan to Beersheba, lived in safety, everyone under their own vine and under their own fig tree." 1 Kings 4:25

Thought

Some countries in the world do better for the well-being and prosperity of their citizens than others. But I do not know of any country that can legitimately be described like Israel and Judah were under the leadership of Solomon at that point in his reign.

Everyone lived in *safety*. That suggests that crime rate was so low it was statistically insignificant and negligible. It is not unusual for the rich, the powerful and the famous to live in safety. They tend to live in neighborhoods where there is adequate protection provided by the government. They often occupy residences that are in gated communities managed by private security personnel. Their houses have alarm systems installed to add an extra layer of protection to their already safe environment. People with means are accustomed to being protected and no one is surprised to read or hear about those people living in safety.

But safety is a bit elusive for people whose living conditions are not fortunate enough to enjoy such benefits. There are many neighborhoods whose relationships with security forces are adversarial. The culture within too many police departments has made our law enforcement officers more like occupying forces, and reducing their presence to that of wardens of community prisons. Containment and punishment seem to be their primary objectives, and protecting the larger society from the people in that section of the community seems to be their goal.

Too often, these are the dynamics in communities of color and low-income neighborhoods. The irony here is that those employed to serve and protect are not safe in this kind of environment themselves. Prejudice, anger and fear often drive their behavior and also influence the conclusions made by these law enforcement personnel. This has contributed to many communities experiencing a tremendous breakdown in safety that has reached very dangerous levels in many American cities.

Where there is no safety, disinvestment occurs. Efforts to revitalize depressed communities necessarily begin with addressing safety issue. Where there is no safety, property values plummet and home ownership are challenging at best. So, where there is no safety, residents have minimum stake in the community, education suffers because students live in fear and education officers are reluctant to work in unsafe environments. The lack of safety makes it almost impossible to create and sustain a sense of community among residents.

Safety is a foundational component of healthy community life. It is not the responsibility of government alone, but to the extent that government uses resources to provide public safety, it is incumbent upon government officials to ensure that the most effectives strategies are being used. It is also incumbent upon citizens to be involved in the planning and execution of safety measures.

Financial freedom is easier to achieve and sustain where everyone lives in safety.

Prayer

God, use me to contribute to the safety of my community.

Decision

Today I have decided to: _____

_____

_____

_____

_____

DAY 7 WIN-WIN

Verse

"In this way, Hiram kept Solomon supplied with all the cedar and juniper logs he wanted, and Solomon gave Hiram twenty thousand cors of wheat as food for his household, in addition to twenty thousand baths of pressed olive oil. Solomon continued to do this for Hiram year after year." 1 Kings 5: 10&11

Thought

When we began organizing efforts to improve the neighborhood surrounding our church, one of our first tasks was to define the area that we understood to be our neighborhood. Not only was there no distinctly obvious way to identify general boundaries, but the greater challenge was that the church was located on a street that divided two different municipalities and two separate counties.

As if this was not complicated enough, the two municipalities were controlled by two different political parties, and thus were governed differently. Needless to say, the two sides of the same street were like two different worlds.

These were not insignificant dynamics because an initiative to revitalize an area around a major thoroughfare requires planning for both sides of the street. Traffic studies, density analyses, crime rates, social service needs and more were all relevant factors for investment and development on both sides. Besides, the church owned property on both sides of the street and understood the neighborhood as being inclusive of both sides.

Our challenge was that we were the only people who saw it that way. The residents on one side did not identify as neighbors to those on the other side. Neither did businesses on one side support those on the other side. And to top it off, the politicians on either side did not communicate. Even the churches on one side kept their distance from churches on the other side. This was a planner's nightmare.

We started holding meetings to discuss the future of the neighborhood using alternate venues on either side of the street for inclusivity. When it was time to meet with the municipal government officials, the two sides quickly recognized the need for additional water supply in one city and the capacity of the other to sell water. They were able to craft a win-win relationship of buying and selling water.

Solomon was wise enough to realize that he needed relationships and partners to accomplish his goals. Not only did he develop a kind of relationship with Hiram, a Phoenician king of Tyre, that benefitted his people, but he also had strong ties to the Lebanese. In fact, Solomon's relationships resulted in many gentiles actually helping him build the Jewish temple.

We must continuously build relationships with people from different backgrounds and persuasions for purposes that can become mutually beneficial. We may find that through such relationships, we create solutions and opportunities that we could not have created by ourselves.

Prayer

God, help me to build win-win relationships.

Decision

Today I have decided to: _____

_____

_____

_____

_____

8 GOD FIRST

Verse

"It took Solomon thirteen years, however, to complete the construction of his palace."
1 Kings 7:1

Thought

It took seven years to build the elaborate temple constructed for the worship of God. When we consider the size and the materials used in constructing the temple, and the fact that the project was done by hand, we can appreciate why it took so long. Anything worth building requires time. Despite the frustration that accompanies prolonged processes, the finished product always makes it worthwhile.

Now the text says that after the temple was built, Solomon spent the next thirteen years constructing his palace. Notice that the verse includes the word "*however*." At first glance this implies a contrast being made between the building of the temple and the building of the palace. And I'm sure there is some significance to the respective duration of each project. But what was striking to me was that King Solomon prioritized building God's house over building his own.

The residence of a royal leader was not simply a place to live. A palace was a place to conduct official state business; the location for receiving and entertaining foreign dignitaries; the symbol of power and prestige. Perhaps that is why kings would build ostentatious palaces – the ultimate international statement.

Solomon was only the third king of this young nation. It made good political sense for him to have a major palace. He was an international figure since his people had become players on the international stage. He had married an Egyptian princess who was accustomed to living in superior royal accommodations. Solomon had no choice but to have a noteworthy palace.

Yet he waited seven years before starting the construction of his palace because he felt that it was more important to build a house for God first.

Putting God first is a common expression used by Christians. Unfortunately, too often, the behavior that accompanies the use of that phase involves regular church attendance and periodic participation in church activities. But Solomon put God first by organizing his agenda, his time, his resources in a way that made his own need for a palace secondary to the need for a temple of God.

If more Christians really did put God first, we would have more church members involved in active ministry. If we really put God first, we would spend much more time in Bible study to understand the principles by which God desires for us to live. If we put God first, we would have no problem with the principle of giving God a tithe of our increase.

Too many Christians believe that the word "*tithe*" means regular giving. But tithe is literally ten percent of our income/increase and we are told to bring the tithe into the storehouse – the church.

Putting God first in our finances makes it more likely that we will put God first in every other aspect of our lives.

Prayer

God, give me the faith that I need to put you first in all that I do.

Decision

Today I have decided to: _____

_____

_____

_____

_____

FORCED LABOR

Verse

"Here is the account of the forced labor King Solomon conscripted to build the Lord's temple, his own palace, the terraces,[f] the wall of Jerusalem, and Hazor, Megiddo and Gezer…"
1 Kings 9:15

Thought

A coach would show his athletic team a video coverage of a previous game, if available, to help them improve or prepare for an encounter with an opponent. This helps the team identify and appreciate specific things they had done well, as well as what needed to be improved in the next game.

It would be demoralizing to show the team footage of only their mistakes. They would think the coach saw nothing good about their performance. Likewise, it would be deceptive to only show the team only clips of their best performances because that would create the false impression that they had no flaws and nothing needed to improve. By exposing the team to both the good and the bad, the coach presents a well-rounded picture of reality while using that to develop a strategy for future victory.

That is a very similar approach to the one used by God in preparing the Bible for us. What I love about the Bible is that the text is not sugar-coated, limited to inspirational stories and moralizing platitudes. Of course, I believe the Bible is the inspired word of God. I also believe the Bible has as many examples of what we should not do, as it does what we should do. We are led by moral principles contained in the Bible without being expected to replicate ancient practices that violate the ethics of Jesus or basic common sense.

One such practice is slavery. Solomon is justifiably admired for many different things – he made building God's temple a priority in an exemplary way; he requested and received wisdom when he had the opportunity to ask the Maker of heaven and earth for anything he desired; and he displayed that wisdom and used Godly judgement when making difficult decisions. He inspired an entire book of wise sayings, many of which are woven into the tapestry of our cultures. But Solomon was the sponsor and practitioner of forced labor. In other words, Solomon used slaves to build the temple and his palace.

There have been different forms of slavery throughout history. Some people go to great lengths to describe the nuances of slavery in its various forms in order to diminish the cruelty factor from place to place. But every form of slavery involved a lessening of status and stripping of some basic human right for the slave! In other words, there is no such thing as good slavery.

Forced labor meant at least two things: 1. The people worked against their will; 2. They were not compensated for their work. Those two factors alone make slavery a miserable condition for the slave. Slavery was abolished much later, but Solomon, in all his glory, like many of our modern American heroes, owned and used slaves. And that was not OK.

Prayer

God, help me to always see and oppose injustice.

Decision

Today I have decided to: _____

_____

_____

_____

_____

QUEEN OF SHEBA

Verse

"And she [Queen of Sheba] gave the king 120 talents of gold, large quantities of spices, and precious stones. Never again were so many spices brought in as those the queen of Sheba gave to King Solomon." I Kings 10:10

Thoughts

World scholars, historians and theologians do not agree on the historicity of the description or identity of the Queen of Sheba. However, there are sufficient references to the mysterious royal woman who visited Solomon to conclude that a significant female personality did actually become a part of King Solomon's legacy, and that this woman was very wealthy and had a dark complexion.

Jewish historian Josephus believed and wrote in his epic work, *Antiquities*, that she was the queen of Egypt and Ethiopia. Tradition says that when she died, she was buried in Nigeria. Many believe that she was actually from a place named Saba in Arabia, and the people of Yemen claim her as theirs. What is even more fascinating is that the Judeo-Christian heritage has maintained that this encounter between a Jewish royal and an African or Arab royal is an important enough narrative to preserve and include in holy texts.

I refer to this as fascinating because the dominant American narratives that describe the history of the country and the history of black people systematically exclude the "Queens of Sheba" in American history. It was more than two hundred years before DNA testing confirmed the relationship between Thomas Jefferson, the third President of the United States, and his enslaved concubine, Sally Hemings, who died in 1835. Not one word about Hemings was ever mentioned in United States history books until the past few years.

After two centuries of denials, cover-ups and disagreements about the nature of Thomas' and Hemings' relationship, the Thomas Jefferson Foundation of Monticello announced the Sally Hemings exhibit. Ms. Hemings never received the acclaim of the Queen of Sheba but she certainly played a significant role in the life of our third president just as the Queen is believed to have impacted the life of Israel's third king.

Perhaps the acceptance of this ancient Queen is attributable to the fact that the Hebrew narrative understands the role that Solomon played in the international arena. Solomon interacted with leaders from non-Jewish nations and had strategic relationships with them. Solomon married an Egyptian princess and had a harem populated by women from many nations. None of this seems to have bothered Jewish sensibilities enough to delete this queen, whose historical identity is questionable, from their Bible and their history.

Like Ruth, whose story will come later, she was able to have a position of literary prominence without being one of their own.

Sally Hemings was a controversial figure in American history and therefore erased as if she did not exist. The rumors about her sexual relationship with Thomas Jefferson were embarrassing because the American narrative could not embrace their interracial affair, even in a period when it was commonly known that white slave owners had intimate relationships with enslaved black women. But her descendants today unearthed the treasures of her legacy. Thank God she made sure her children knew her story.

Prayer

Dear God, help me to know, remember and share my own story.

Decision:

Today I have decided to: _____

_____

_____

_____

_____

LYING PROPHETS

Verse

"The old prophet answered, "I too am a prophet, as you are. And an angel said to me by the word of the Lord: 'Bring him back with you to your house so that he may eat bread and drink water.'" (But he was lying to him)."
1 Kings 13:18

Thought

I visited an African nation during my sabbatical and had one of the best trips of my life. I had never been to this country and knew absolutely no one there. I had gotten the name of one person from a friend of mine at the United Nations and that person never showed up to pick me up from the airport when I arrived. But it was still a marvelous trip.

I visited a newly opened stock exchange and addressed a group of college students who were there learning about investing. I also met a woman who had been selected to be the first female chief in the history of the country. These were some of the most intriguing days I have ever spent anywhere.

I was invited to have lunch with a group of men who were civil servants working in various sectors of the government. We had a pleasant conversation about their work and I answered numerous questions about my time in various government positions. Then the conversation got serious.

They had selected one of their colleagues to be the "spokesman" for the next part of our conversation. They were all very concerned about clergy from another country in Africa, whom they said were preying on vulnerable women in their country. They were referring to ministers that we call "prosperity preachers" whose message is essentially that if the people will have faith and give them their money, then God would in turn make them wealthy.

It seemed this country was specifically targeted because it was relatively better off economically than many other sub-Saharan nations. There was a parade of preachers who were drawing thousands of people to stadiums and convincing them to give money and valuables to show their faith in God.

Having heard my message about using credit wisely, saving for emergencies and investing in assets that grow, they were initially skeptical. They knew I was a minister from the United States and they were waiting for my "prosperity gimmick." All they knew about preachers was that they all had get-rich-quick schemes, but the only people that got rich were the preachers themselves!

I assured them that I had no gimmick and that there were many honest preachers. Then I also had the unenviable task of warning them that there were, indeed, many lying prophets and preachers.

In our verse, this old prophet tricked the younger man of God into going to his house to eat when God told him to do otherwise. That was a fatal decision. But he was deceived by a prophet – a *lying* prophet.

Not all preachers can be trusted. Not all sermons are true. If the young prophet had done what he knew God had instructed, he would have fared much better. When we do what the Bible says to do and use common sense, no lying prophet will be able to get us into financial trouble.

Prayer

Dear God, help me to discern the lying prophet.

Decision

Today I have decided to: _____

_____

_____

_____

_____

EXCELLENT WORK

Verse

"Now Jeroboam was a man of standing: and when Solomon saw how well the young man did his work, he put him in charge of the whole labor force of the tribes of Joseph."
1 Kings 11:28 NIV.

Thought

This is not a very inspiring chapter of the Bible, nor is it a high point in Solomon's life. In this chapter, the writer describes the king's lack of devotion for God, starting with his marriage to 700 foreign wives. Solomon had begun worshipping the pagan gods of the nations of his many wives.

His father, David, had committed murder in order to eliminate the husband of the woman that he desired. In spite of the severity of David's sin, Solomon was described in verse 6 as having done "… *evil in the eyes of the Lord; he did not follow the Lord completely as David his father had done.*" 1 Kings 11:6

God was so displeased with Solomon that God promised to tear the kingdom away from him and give it to one of his subordinates (verse 11).

But right there in the middle of this narrative where we are witnesses to the demise of Solomon and the surging of his enemies, we also see a quick glimpse of a critical principle. The drama is thickening – the enemies are rising. Then Solomon actually promotes his soon-to-become adversary because he saw how well the young man did his work. Solomon put him in charge.

During the Jim Crow era, when black people were freer than they were in slavery but still lived under very explicit restrictions, embedded in the culture of black people was a passionate commitment to excellence. Black parents and black leaders were not naïve concerning the depth of racist belief that existed in America. Black people knew that whites had been convinced that black people were not fully human. Black people understood full well that white Christians believed that God had ordained black people to serve white people. And black people also knew that blacks had to be strategic in order to matriculate into the American society and enjoy full citizenship. There was no doubt that this would not be easy.

Therefore, one of the most important beliefs was that if black people performed with excellence, it would force white society to re-think its racist assumptions and respect blacks for their undeniable achievements in every field of endeavor. That perspective was not limited to sports and entertainment only; black excellence was promoted in science, education, business, law, medicine, finance and every conceivable industry.

The strategy of using excellence as a response to racism is still effective today. No legislation will ever be as effective in changing the hearts and minds of racists as will the excellent work performed by a black person in an area that blacks were considered incapable. Excellence is the cure for race and gender bias and ignorance.

Prayer

God, give me the strength to pursue and achieve excellence.

Decision

Today I have decided to: _____

_____

_____

_____

_____

UNUSUAL FAITH

Verse

"She went away and did as Elijah had told her. So, there was food every day for Elijah and for the woman and her family." 1 Kings 17:15

Thought

Elijah was a prophet that God called to challenge the corrupt leadership of King Ahab. Although he is clearly the main character of this narrative, a poor widow demonstrates such unusual faith that, at minimum, she qualifies for a "best supporting" role.

As a widow, she was certainly in a poor financial condition. Since women were not allowed to own land and had no real social status in the ancient culture, this widow was at the bottom of the socio-economic structure. As a single mother, she had the added burden of providing for a son from her meager means. We can see how poor she was by her description of herself when Elijah asked her for water and a piece of bread. She told him that she had only enough to make one meal, after which she and her son would lay down and die.

Her poverty was not only caused by her lack of support from a husband, but also by the drought that had impacted the entire country. God had used ravens to feed Elijah when he camped by the Brook of Cherith before it dried up and he moved on. That means that Elijah was actually in a much better shape than the widow when they met. He probably didn't have any signs of being as hungry as she was, and he only asked for a piece of bread, suggesting that he likely just wanted "a little something to take the edge off", as my wife would say.

The widow was gathering sticks to make a fire and fix a meal. Yet despite her hunger, she was willing to provide for a complete stranger before addressing her own needs and her son's. That is unusual faith!

I call it faith because Elijah had told her the God of Israel promised that if she provided for him, her flour and oil would last throughout the drought. She had no basis for believing that was true. That is faith – believing something without having any factual basis for it. I also call it faith because this woman referred to God as Elijah's God, meaning she was trusting the God that Elijah served, who was not necessarily her God.

Our faith in God is often formed and nurtured based on the experiences, testimonies and faith of others. Elijah's confidence in God's promise provoked this widow to demonstrate such unusual faith that she indeed qualifies to win the "best supporting" award.

Not only is her faith exemplary, it is also challenging. She gave her best because she gave her last. Giving the only something we have in service to someone else and in response to God's promise is unusual. She may never hear these words but clearly, she believed that it is truly better to give than to receive.

Prayer

God, increase my faith.

Decision

Today I have decided to: _____

_____

_____

_____

_____

RESOURCEFUL LEADERSHIP

Verse

"While Jezebel was killing off the Lord's prophets, Obadiah had taken a hundred prophets and hidden them in two caves, fifty in each, and had supplied them with food and water."
1 Kings 18:4 NIV

Thought

When I was a child, I didn't know why many of my friends thought that my family was wealthy. We lived on the second floor of a three-story house that was owned by my maternal grandmother in the "colored" section of town. My father was an eighth grade English teacher and my mother was a secretary. This is where we lived until I was 10, and then we moved into a very modest three-bedroom house in the same town.

School teachers and secretaries did not make a lot of money. We certainly were not poor, but we were also nowhere near wealthy. The reason my friends thought we were rich was because my father was also a minister – the pastor of a small church in town.

Black ministers were men (very few women clergy in those days) who were highly respected in our communities. Many black leaders elected to public office were members of the clergy; prominent civil rights leaders were mostly clergy; and many of the fine homes and nice cars belonged to black ministers. Pastors of black churches were some of the most visible and admired men in black communities, and with that admiration came the assumption that all black preachers were wealthy.

While a handful of black clergymen throughout the country were relatively well-off financially, most back then were bi-vocational as they are today. They made a living doing their nine-to-five jobs, and they received "love gifts" or stipends for their church work. My dad was one.

Every minister I ever met dreamt of being able to work for the church full time. Like my dad, they were committed to serving God in fulltime ministries with parttime salaries. They would use sick days and vacation time from their regular jobs to cover church responsibilities like funerals.

Most black pastors had no retirement savings and could never afford to retire and collect a pension from their churches. For vacations, they attended church conventions.

Now we read that Obadiah was a prophet. Obadiah also worked in the Ahab administration. Today, we would describe him as being bi-vocational. He worked for the government as palace administrator and for God as a leader and spokesman.

He probably earned more money working for Ahab than he did working for God.

When Queen Jezebel threatened to kill Israel's prophets, Obadiah was able to hide one hundred of them in two caves and provide food and water for all of them for as long as they were in hiding.

The moral of this story for clergy and church leaders: there is nothing wrong with having the means to provide for others as a leader in the church. Even if it means having a real job! Someone has to have the resources, monetary or other, to ensure that God's work is carried out successful.

Prayer

God, help me to avoid feeling guilty for having the means to provide for others.

Decision

Today I have decided to: _____

_____

_____

_____

_____

YOUR INHERITANCE

Verse

But Naboth replied, "The Lord forbid that I should give you the inheritance of my ancestors." 1 Kings 21:3 NIV

Thought

Every human being receives an inheritance at birth. Whenever a baby is born, they inherit something from their parents, often their physical features. I am always interested in seeing pictures of parents when they were the age of their children. In some cases, even they cannot distinguish themselves from their children.

We also inherit style from our parents. I always blame my near obsession with matching my clothes and making sure my attire is impeccable on my mother. My dad had a tremendous influence also, as he always laid out his clothes the night before he planned to wear them. As much as I resented their scrutiny of what I was wearing, they left me an inheritance of understanding the phrase "dress for success" that has served me well.

We also inherit values from our parents. Sometimes as we age and mature, we actually discover that we value music, art, food and ideas that we did not realize that we did. The exposures of our youth and the impressions made on us contribute significantly to who we become. I consider emotional, religious, and social values very concrete inheritances.

Of course, we certainly inherit assets from our parents and our families. The first home that I owned, I inherited from my grandmother. In fact, she transferred ownership to my uncle and me before she died to spare us any legal complications after she died. And that one inheritance got me started toward ownership of multiple properties, including some investment properties.

King Ahab desired to own a vineyard that was owned by a man named Naboth. Today we would call Ahab's offer to replace Naboth's vineyard with a better vineyard or purchase it at a great price "eminent domain." Much of the urban gentrification that has dislocated many urban poor people has been facilitated by government use of eminent domain, which allows the government to seize property from owners. Throughout the south, many black families sold land voluntarily – often children who inherited land from parents. Naboth said no.

Naboth's "no" was rooted in his commitment to honoring his ancestors. He believed that to allow the king to have his vineyard would be to dishonor his ancestors. His ancestors had worked hard to build and sustain that vineyard; they had been diligent in protecting it; and they had made the necessary provisions to pass that vineyard on to future generations.

So, the Naboth mentality says that we should both value our inheritances and leave an inheritance of value. Whether they are cultural or financial, we should understand our inheritance as blessings that cannot be dishonored or abandoned, even when pressured by political or governmental powers. Naboth stood his ground and gave his life for his commitment, but his legacy will inspire us to protect what we inherit.

Prayer

God, help me to appreciate and protect what I have inherited from my ancestors.

Decision

Today I have decided to: _____

_____

_____

_____

_____

SPECIAL POWER

Verse

When they had crossed, Elijah said to Elisha, "Tell me, what can I do for you before I am taken from you?" "Let me inherit a double portion of your spirit," Elisha replied. 2 Kings 2:9 NIV.

Thought

When someone succeeds another person in a job or a position in which the predecessor has had tremendous success, the successor is often described as having "big shoes to fill." In other words, the achievements of the predecessor were so significant that the person following that success has to work very hard to match or exceed the accomplishments.

God had used the prophet Elijah to do things no previous prophet had ever done. Elijah's successor, Elisha, was following a man who terrified King Ahab and Queen Jezebel, defeated hundreds of Baal's prophets on Mt. Carmel, raised a dead boy back to life, and oversaw a miraculous provision of food and oil for a widow and her son. Elijah could have been considered a super prophet!

Now here came Elisha who had been very pleased to serve Elijah. Once Elijah was taken to heaven by God in a chariot of fire, it was time for Elisha to represent God in the same way as his predecessor. But how would he do it?

Elijah asked Elisha what he could do for him before he departed this world. This was a similar question to the one God asked Solomon just as he was becoming king. Solomon asked for wisdom for the many decisions he would have to make as leader of the kingdom. But the job of the prophet was not to manage the kingdom, but to declare God's word and will for the people. That required more than wisdom – that required power.

The most important kind of power needed to accomplish great deeds is power that cannot be gotten from titles, positions, money, or government. Elisha understood that he needed a unique kind of power. We, too, should recognize that our ability to sustain any of our accomplishments or achieve new ones requires a unique kind of internal power.

I received a call from a friend one morning to tell me about a significant business development that had recently occurred for them. It was really big news! We discussed the potential implications of what had happened. I was complimentary and celebrative on their behalf, and thrilled for my friend's breakthrough.

Later that day, I received a text message from the same friend telling me that their 31-year-old son had been found dead in a hotel room not too long after our marvelous call that morning.

This would be their second loss of a child, and there is no business deal in the world that can satisfy the emotional, spiritual, and psychological needs of a parent who must endure the ordeal of burying their child, much less two.

Elisha knew that Elijah had faced death and experienced loneliness, depression, doubt, and despair, all while being used to reveal and demonstrate God's power. So, he didn't ask for Elijah's chariot or wardrobe or any of his physical possessions. Elisha asked for a double portion of the power that made Elijah so effective throughout his prophetic career. That power was in Elijah's spirit.

Prayer

God, please strengthen my spirit.

Decision

Today I have decided to: _____

_____

_____

_____

_____

POURING OIL

Verse

*She went and told the man of God, and he said,
"Go, sell the oil and pay your debts. You and
your sons can live on what is left."*
2 Kings 4:7 NIV

Thought

I am often asked for advice about investing money, and I am always quick to remind the enquirer that I am not a financial professional. I am neither licensed to sell financial products nor offer investment advice. I believe everyone should have a financial adviser who is, at least, a Certified Financial Planner (CFP) because although CFPs are not licensed to sell products either, they are licensed to assist with financial planning, which may lead to purchasing financial products such as insurance, mutual funds, and more.

What I know about money I learned from being broke, being tired of being broke and seeking every ounce of information I could find to change my financial status. I started by changing my mentality about spending, beginning with the way I used credit cards and debt.

I am not opposed to using debt as a means of creating wealth. I was using credit to fund a lifestyle that I could not afford. When my salary was $25,000 a year, I had a credit card with a $5,000 credit limit and I used that card to supplement my salary, living and spending as if I earned $30,000 a year!

I learned that the best investment for me to make was to pay off my credit cards and their high interests, and start investing in assets that grow. After I got out of debt, I started to put aside a little money at a time and invest in stocks and real estate. I started with very small amounts.

Our subject in the verse is woman whose husband had died and left her with a lot of debt. Her creditors threatened to enslave her two sons if she didn't pay, but all she had was a small jar of oil. When she turned to Prophet Elisha, he advised her to borrow some pots and start pouring the oil into the pots. As the woman did this, the oil never ceased to flow and she was able to sell the oil to pay off her debts.

The incessant pouring of the little oil she had should inspire us to invest a little of what we have into strategies that grow our money into multiple streams of income. You would be surprised at how a little money placed into the right places consistently over a period of time can grow into such value that we are able to liquidate at some point to take care of major responsibilities.

Note, however, that the woman first had to pour her oil before she could profit from it. You probably have some oil you can pour that can turn into profits.

Prayer

God, show me where to pour my oil.

Decision

Today I have decided to: _____

_____

_____

_____

_____

OWNERSHIP MATTERS

Verse

"Let's make a small room on the roof and put in it a bed and a table, a chair and a lamp for him. Then he can stay there whenever he comes to us." 2 Kings 4:10

Thought

My maternal grandmother was the "church mother" at the Trinity Temple Church of God in Christ in the 1960s. In this role, she had tremendous influence in the church. I strongly believe that the tradition of church mother derives from the role of Queen Mother in West Africa. In both instances, this designation is taken very seriously both by the person who holds it and her community.

Just as the African Queen Mother has a close relationship with the African King, so does the church mother have a close working relationship with the Pastor of a church. My grandmother's pastor was Bishop Frederick Douglas Washington, one of the most renowned preachers among black Pentecostal Christians. As a child, I hated Bishop Washington!

There was a wooden cabinet in my grandmother's dining room that had a glass door and through it remained permanently visible glasses, dishes, plates, forks and knives that could not be touched. They were reserved for Bishop Washington's use only. The Bishop obliged himself to use those well-protected items every Sunday after church services when he would come to our house for a sumptuous meal prepared by my grandmother.

Grandma had the kind of respect and admiration for her Bishop that the Shunammite woman had for the prophet Elisha. She was married and quite well-to-do, and whenever Elisha was in Shunem, he would go to her house for dinner, just like Bishop Washington would come to ours. The woman concluded that Elisha was a Holy Man and suggested to her husband that they build an extra room in their house so they could provide Elisha with lodging when he needed it. They did exactly that, and Elisha accepted their offer and embraced their hospitality.

Her love and admiration for Prophet Elisha was sincere and generous, but her ability to actually provide support for Elisha and his cause was due to the fact that she and her husband owned their own home and could do with it whatever they chose. One very important resource to have is to be in a position to support important causes in tangible ways.

Many admirable Christian leaders have taken vows of poverty and have renounced all earthly ownership. But many Christian causes and Christian institutions have been made possible by the generosity of people with means. When we own assets, we have the option to do more than just pray for people and projects that we love and support. We can make those resources available to protect the church and its leaders from begging for support and perhaps even compromising their principles in order to make ends meet.

Both Elisha and Bishop Washington had physical nurture and people with means who made places for them in the homes that they owned.

Prayer

God, help me become an owner of resources that can be used to support ministry.

Decision

Today I have decided to: _____

_____

_____

_____

_____

DISABILITY INSURANCE

Verse

"Now Naaman was commander of the army of the king of Aram. He was a great man in the sight of his master and highly regarded, because through him the Lord had given victory to Aram. He was a valiant soldier, but he had leprosy." 2 Kings 6:1 NIV

Thought

I discovered early in my work that many people within the financial services industry needed as much help with their personal finances as everyone else.

I already had great appreciation for the need for insurance. Of course, auto insurance is mandatory almost everywhere, so I have always had insurance for my car since I started driving at 17. I also knew that life insurance was important to have; my grandmother got a weekly visit from an insurance agent to whom she paid her premium and my father had a part time job selling life insurance for the black-owned North Carolina Mutual Life Insurance Company. When my father died at age 47, he was well insured. That is how I grew into adulthood embracing insurance products as a necessity and not a luxury.

I learned an alarming fact during the first workplace presentation I made of my dfree® program to a New England insurance company. I would fly out to their headquarters once a week to present to their employees. It was through my work with the employees of this company that I learned that I could more likely become disabled before age 65 than die before that age. This stunned me! I had never given any thought to being disabled before age 65.

Shortly after this newfound knowledge, a dear friend of mine became too sick to work. In fact, he had been a successful professional and an active man who played golf, travelled extensively and was well-respected among our peers. In many ways, he was like Naaman who also was a great man and highly regarded. He was too young to retire but he had never purchased disability insurance. Like Naaman, he had a "but" at the end of his bio. Naaman was great, *but* he was a leper. My friend was great, *but* he was disabled.

To be without an income is devastating. To be incapable of earning an income can be fatal. The best way to protect our income and our assets is to purchase insurance, including disability insurance. This must be a part of your budget; take the time to find the right policy and buy it. If you already have it, then check to make sure you have sufficient amount. This is an aspect of health insurance that we ignore too often.

As grandma would say, "*It's better to have it and not need it, than to need it and not have it.*"

Prayer

God, please keep me healthy and give me the common sense to secure disability insurance.

Decision

Today I have decided to: _____

_____

_____

_____

_____

BORROWED STUFF

Verse

As one of them was cutting down a tree, the iron axhead fell into the water. "Oh no, my lord!" he cried out. "It was borrowed!" 2 Kings 6:5 NIV

Thought

I once bought a leather jacket that I believed made me the best dressed person in my high school. It took me a year to save enough for it and when I finally had the money, I went confidently to the clothing store and it became mine.

This was not something my parents were willing to spend money on because it was certainly not a necessity. My brother and I learned at an early age that there was a stark difference between things that we wanted and what we needed.

We always had what we needed – food, clothing and shelter – but extravagances were not a part of our childhood experience. We had a clear understanding that when our father simply did not respond to a request, it must mean it was for something desired but not needed.

I had worked part-time delivering take-out chicken dinners and saved all the money I made, including birthday gifts from relatives, until I had sufficient funds to buy that special leather jacket. When I took it home, I hung it on my bedroom door so I could look at it while I lay in my bed. I loved the jacket so much that there was no occasion or destination worthy of my wearing it. So, it ended up hanging on the door until the most popular guy in our class invited me to an "exclusive" party at his house – well, his parents' house!

I could tell it was great party when I arrived. Several cars lined the cul-de-sac, and the music could be heard from the street. There were a few guys on the steps trying to negotiate access into the party even though they were not invited. One of them reached past my friend at the door, grabbed something from the hallway and ran into the street. As my friend started to go after him in the cold winter night, he asked for my jacket and I gave it to him – reluctantly.

It was like a movie scene as he grabbed the door of the car the guys were in and they dragged my friend along all the way down the street. Needless to say, by the time he returned to the house, his clothes were ripped to shreds – including my beautiful, brand new jacket!! Apparently, it never occurred to him that he was wearing a borrowed item that required extra care.

Prayer

God, help me to respect and protect other people's possessions as if they were my own.

Decision

Today I have decided to: _____

_____

_____

_____

_____

DAY 21 HIGH PRICES

Verse

"Sometime later, Ben-Hadad, king of Aram mobilized his entire army and marched up and laid siege to Samaria. There was a great famine in the city; the siege lasted so long that a donkey's head sold for eighty shekels of silver, and a quarter of a cab of seed pods for five shekels." 2 Kings 6:24 & 25 NIV

Thought

I'm sure none of us are accustomed to negotiating the purchase of a donkey's head or seed pods, but almost all of us can recount a time when the prices we paid for goods and services were significantly less than we pay today. When I tell young audiences that $1 worth of gasoline was enough to last me an entire week, they think I am 150 years old.

Inflation is a reality that impacts almost every facet of our lives. Of course, technology has reversed many inflationary trends and there are certain devices and products we can purchase today for significantly less money. My first digital high-definition TV cost me ten times more than I recently paid for an HD flat screen smart TV, and my desktop printer in my home office was cheaper than my first laser printer.

But the commodities that we need to survive and the products that we purchase to meet our everyday needs have a tendency to get more and more expensive. That is inflation, and that is what the Samaritans were experiencing due to famine and war.

People suffer in ways that cannot be described when natural disasters occur. If a fruit-growing region has unusually cold weather, it can affect the harvest and the distribution, and finally the sale and consumption of the fruit. That is a chain effect.

Wars have the same dynamic. The mere threat of war can affect the travel and hospitality industry, the food industry, the housing industry and the entertainment industry. I am certain that very few international travelers took vacations in Afghanistan during the past twenty years, and no one, except essential personnel, traveled during the early months of the COVID-19 pandemic.

But guess who did very well in Samaria during the famine and the war? Those who sold donkey heads and seed pods! The message is this: there is always someone making a profit no matter the conditions. We should constantly be looking for investment opportunities that offer a healthy return for strategic investing during challenging times.

Good financial professionals can assist us in making that happen. That is what they do.

Prayer

God, open my eyes that I might see opportunities during challenging times.

Decision

Today I have decided to: _____

_____

_____

_____

_____

CLERGY
ACCOUNTABILITY

Verse

Therefore, King Joash summoned Jehoiada, the priest, and the other priests and asked them, "Why aren't you repairing the damage done to the temple? Take no more money from your treasurers, but hand it over for repairing the temple." 2 Kings 12:7 NIV

Thought

A clergyman recently admitted to stealing more than a half million dollars from his church collections. The members of the congregation were understandably shocked and angry to learn that their beloved pastor, who had served them for many years, had violated their trust in that manner.

Financial support for churches and other ministries is a spiritual act of faith. People who give tithes and offerings do so because they love God and believe in the ministry they are supporting. While it is true that givers are giving to God, there is an expectation that the funds that are given will be used for very specific ministry activities and operations. It is not practical for every individual to participate in managing the use of church monies. That is why churches and religious organizations have boards and committees that supervise the use of funds they collect. It is also why church leaders report periodically to their members and supporters on the use of funds over certain periods of time.

One of the most damaging occurrences in any organization is to discover that there has been some misappropriation or mismanagement of resources, and rightly so. People work long, hard hours to earn their livelihoods. The last thing they need is to discover that the ministry they give freely to has allowed their donations to be misused.

What is even more inappropriate is for church leaders to tell their members that because they are "giving to God", they cannot question the use of funds once the gift changes hands. It is also abusive to claim that the tithe belongs to God and therefore no one has the right to question how the church uses it.

Joash was a young king, but still king enough to know that there was something seriously wrong with how the priests were diverting funds meant for the repair of the temple! And he did something about it. He gave orders that ensured that the funds were redirected back the temple works.

As leaders of congregations, clergy must be accountable for leading in a manner that assures supporters that their ministries operate with fiscal integrity. People must require proof of that kind of structure before joining or continuing their financial support of any ministry.

Prayer

God, give me the courage to ask questions about the finances that I donate to ministry.

Decision

Today I have decided to: _____

_____

_____

_____

_____

23 LIVING WILL

Verse

In those days, Hezekiah became ill and was at the point of death. The prophet Isaiah, son of Amoz, went to him and said, "This is what the Lord says: Put your house in order, because you are going to die; you will not recover."
2 Kings 20:1 NIV

Thought

Medical technology has made it possible for people to live far beyond their natural years. One of the most difficult decisions for a family to make involves how long to keep a loved one on life support. Circumstances requiring such decisions are now widespread within hospitals and the health care system due to the existence of very sophisticated technologies.

When making these decisions, it is important to develop some consensus about the definition of the word "life". We are often called upon to determine various degrees and levels of the "quality of life." Despite many efforts to create tools that can measure this, more often than not the conclusions drawn from these instruments can be quite subjective and not always helpful. I have witnessed families have such difficulty deciding on the appropriate treatment for a loved one that the disagreement does irreparable harm to their relationships.

King Hezekiah was not on life support but he had an illness that the prophet Isaiah predicted would end his life. Hezekiah followed up the prophet's prediction by going straight to God with a request to live longer, and God granted the king 15 more years. But eventually, he still died.

Isaiah gave him good advice regardless of whether he died then or lived 15 more years. "*Put your house in order*" is good advice whenever it is given because every one of us will face the inevitable end of our physical lives and we might even have our lives extended by machines.

Putting your house in order includes creating written instructions concerning your desires should a time arrive when you cannot make and communicate decisions for yourself about medical treatment. These instructions are living wills and advance directives.

These are written, legal instructions regarding your preferences for medical care if you are unable to make decisions for yourself. Advance directives guide choices for doctors and caregivers if you're terminally ill, seriously injured, in a coma, in the late stages of dementia or near the end of your life.

Advance directives aren't just for older adults. Unexpected end-of-life situations can happen at any age, so it's important for all adults to prepare these documents.

By getting your house in order, you can get the medical care you want, avoid unnecessary suffering and relieve caregivers of decision-making burdens during moments of crisis or grief. You also help reduce confusion or disagreement about the choices you would want people to make on your behalf.

Prayer

God, help me prepare a living will and advance directive.

Decision

Today I have decided to: _____
_____
_____
_____
_____

Verse

Now there were four men with leprosy at the entrance of the city gate. They said to each other, "Why stay here until we die?"
2 Kings 7:3 NIV

Thought

When I was stuck financially and still using my deceased father's American Express card, I saw no light at the end of the tunnel. But my grandmother died and left me 50% ownership of one of her houses and I made the decision that I was going to do something to change my financial life.

I was not sure what I was going to do, but I resolved to change. I was a minister and community leader living above my means. I was challenging political and economic systems to treat black people better while I was ignoring how I treated myself. I was also engaged to be married but too broke to say "I do." My life looked good from the outside but it was quite messy on the inside.

Every option that I considered either seemed impossible to pursue or led to a dead end, and I was uncomfortable asking anyone for advice. It never occurred to me that a legitimate professional of any kind would be obligated to keep my information confidential. Since I had an image to protect (so I thought), I felt that talking to someone would expose me to public embarrassment.

Then I remembered these four lepers. They were sick with a debilitating physical condition but still had somewhat of an advantage over me. They were lepers, they knew they were lepers and everyone else knew that they had leprosy. In that sense they had nothing to hide.

Exposure can be liberating. I have heard executives who've committed crimes say that they actually felt relief after their crimes were discovered and their charade came to an end. These men with leprosy had no need for a cover up and that allowed them the freedom to decide to do something about their situation.

The choice they faced directly addressed the "do nothing and you will die or try something and you could live" notion. In other words, if they tried something, it may or may not work, but if they did nothing, their death was certain.

That was my perspective also. If I did nothing, I could possibly live the rest of my life running from bill collectors and living paycheck to paycheck – I would live in a state of financial death. So, I opted to do something. I attended a free seminar on how to buy houses with no down payment. Instead of paying almost a thousand dollars to attend training, I went to the library and read a book for free and trained myself. I used the strategy in the book, bought my first house without a down payment, sold the house a year later and made enough profit to buy another one. I was on my way.

Every day of my life, I invite someone to do something about their finances. And if they don't know what to do, I also offer them options to access free resources. I am a witness that doing something can yield results.

Prayer

God, give me the courage to do something about my finances.

Decision

Today I have decided to: _____

_____

_____

_____

_____

DAY
25
ECONOMIC JUSTICE

Verse

The king asked the woman about it, and she told him. Then he assigned an official to her case and said to him, "Give back everything that belonged to her, including all the income from her land from the day she left the country until now." 2 Kings 8:6 NIV

Thought

On Sunday December 7, 1941, the Imperial Japanese Navy Air Service executed an attack on the United States naval base at Pearl Harbor in Honolulu, Hawaii. That attack was precipitated by Japan's desire to contain America's Pacific Fleet and to limit their ability to interfere with Japanese military plans in Southeast Asia. 2,403 Americans were killed and 1,178 others were wounded.

In response to this attack, President Franklin D. Roosevelt ordered that Japanese Americans living on the West Coast be placed into concentration camps. Basically, these were prison camps that placed Japanese people in government custody as if they had committed crimes. The perspective that motivated this action was that Japanese people in the United States could be more loyal to the Japanese Empire than to the United States of America during a war between the two countries.

There were some 127,000 people of Japanese ancestry living in the United States at the time. 112,000 that lived on the West Coast were incarcerated as a result of President Roosevelt's Executive Order 9066, which authorized the Secretary of War to prescribe certain areas as military zones, clearing the way for the incarceration of Japanese Americans during the war. About 30,000 of those interned were children!

In response to this racist, immoral act committed against Japanese Americans, the United States government eventually disbursed more than $1.6 billion (equivalent to $3,500,000,000 in 2020) in reparations to 82,219 Japanese Americans who had been incarcerated.

The Shunamite woman in the verse had not been the victim of any injustice, but had been exposed to hard times due to famine. Still, the king had empathy for her circumstances and assigned an official to restore her land and her income the she had lost. This was a just act of the king.

Black Americans worked as enslaved people from 1619 to 1865. A just act would be for the same government that allowed and enabled their oppression to do for them what the United States government did for the Japanese victims, and what the king did for the Shunamite woman – economic justice!

But that is not likely to occur. Therefore, it makes sense for Black Americans to do whatever we can to grow our own wealth and pay reparations to ourselves!

Prayer

God, help me to do for myself what no one is likely to do for me.

Decision

Today I have decided to: _____

_____

_____

_____

_____

HONESTY PAYS

Verse

"But they need not account for the money entrusted to them, because they are honest in their dealings." 2 Kings 22:7 NIV.

Thought

A long time ago, we regularly used the expression *"word is bond."* This expression has woven its way into the tapestry of contemporary culture and a version of it has been used in speeches by First Ladies of the United States of America. The principle embedded in this short phrase is that one's word can be trusted and the implication is that trust has value.

It is certainly true that mistrust can contribute to the erosion of any relationship. Where there is no trust, resources are wasted on monitoring the behavior of people who are suspected to be untrustworthy. Where there is no trust, interaction between people is highly guarded and people are unlikely to form genuine bonds. Where there is no trust, no economic system is sustainable since the exchange of goods and services requires a certain baseline of trust.

What would happen if we could not trust the mechanics who ensure that aircrafts are fit to fly? How would we live if we could not trust medical professionals to serve at the highest levels of proficiency? What happens when a citizenry loses its ability to trust their public officials? Trust matters!

But trust is bred by honesty. The lack of honesty and integrity create the climate of distrust. The king trusted the workers because they were "*honest in their dealings*." That means that these men had displayed honesty over a long enough period of time to cause the king to have full trust in them. They did the work they were hired to do. They also displayed trustworthiness in other areas of their lives because he included, "*in their dealings*."

When a person is honest and trustworthy in one area, it is easy to trust him or her in other areas, too. That is the underlying premise of how businesses, especially lenders, use the credit score. When lenders see our credit score, they make assumptions about the likelihood of our making timely payments if they decided to lend us money. Employers also use credit score to help form impressions of prospective employees.

Although significantly flawed and consistently imperfect, the emphasis on these scores is really an emphasis on honesty and whether or not people will keep their word. When we appear to be honest, we will find that honesty pays.

Prayer

God, help me to be honest in all of my dealings. Amen.

Decision

Today I have decided to: _____

_____

_____

_____

_____

PAYING TAXES

Verse

"Jehoiakim paid Pharaoh Necho the silver and gold he demanded. In order to do so, he taxed the land and exacted the silver and gold from the people of the land according to their assessments." 2 Kings 23:35 NIV

Thought

One of the most humbling experiences I have ever had was when the Internal Revenue Service (IRS) took money out of my bank account to pay income taxes that I owed. I was making a decent amount of money as a public speaker. When the organizations for which I spoke compensated me, they paid me a fee but did not withhold taxes as an employer would. They, however, reported the payment to the IRS.

As I was a self-employed, independent contractor, I was responsible for paying my own taxes. But in those days, I spent all of the money that I earned as soon as I earned it. In fact, I spent a lot of money before I earned it because I used credit cards to finance a lifestyle that exceeded my income. I didn't put any funds aside towards my income taxes; nor did I make quarterly estimated tax payments to the IRS. So, when April 15 came, I didn't have any money to pay the taxes required of me.

I lived this way for a few years until the IRS decided that since I had refused to pay them, they would come and get their money anyway – plus interest and late fees.

I learned a few lessons from that embarrassing and humiliating moment:

1. I file my tax return even if I don't have money to pay IRS the taxes I owe. There is a specific penalty for not filing the tax return in addition to the penalty for not paying the taxes.
2. If the IRS sends me a letter, I respond as soon as possible. They don't take kindly to people who ignore them.
3. If I owe more money than I have, I contact the IRS to arrange a payment plan.
4. I stay faithful to the terms of the payment plan.
5. I make quarterly estimated payments to avoid the financial stress of April 15.
6. If I apply for an extension to file my returns, I understand that I still have to pay the amount of taxes due.

Jehoiakim taxed his citizens to finance Pharaoh Necho's levy on Judah. This was a political arrangement that did not benefit the people in any way. In fact, the levy was imposed after Pharaoh ousted the previous king and appointed Jehoiakim in his place. The people ended up paying for the political debt caused by their leaders.

We are often required to pay taxes to support government policies that we don't support. I have learned that there are many ways we can voice our displeasure with government policies. Withholding our taxes is not one of them.

Prayer

God, help me to avoid trouble with the IRS.

Decision

Today I have decided to: _____

_____

_____

_____

_____

ELIMINATING POVERTY

Verse

*"He [King Nebuchadnezzar] carried all
Jerusalem into exile: all the officers and fighting
men, and all the skilled workers and artisans —
a total of ten thousand. Only the poorest people
of the land were left."* 2 Kings 24:14 NIV

Thought

One of the most persistent questions facing the modern world
is how to eliminate poverty. A visitor from another planet
would have to be baffled by the wealth gap that exists globally
between rich people and poor people, and the gap is getting
wider and wider. I personally know some individuals whose
personal wealth exceeds that of the combined wealth of some
countries' population!

There is no shortage of opinions concerning the solution to this
nagging problem – and it is a problem. A security problem.
History has proven that large concentrations of impoverished
people represent a threat to long term social stability. There is
a limit to the length of time populations will tolerate the living
conditions in poverty-stricken communities.

Poverty is a macroeconomic problem. Countries have greater economic and financial risks when large percentages of their people live in poverty. The cost of managing the social safety net, or the lack thereof, is exponentially higher when growing numbers of people are needy. Not to mention that prisons, schools and healthcare costs to governments are uncontrollable when people without financial means stress those and other systems.

Poverty is also a moral problem. The fact that so many people have no access to a means out of poverty while so many of the wealthy have been able to use societal opportunities to rise to their financial status is indicative of flawed, bias systems. Typically, access to education and training are two major factors that determine economic outcomes for everyone.

Consider what happened when Jerusalem was invaded by the Babylonians; the Temple of God was ransacked and people were taken into exile. Look at the description of who was taken – officers, fighting men, skilled workers and artisans. Who was left behind? The poorest people of the land. In other words, before the invasion, the poorest people were the unskilled and untrained, and that is what we find today all over the world.

Many people believe the redistribution of wealth is the preferred solution to ending poverty. Unless someone's wealth was gained illegally, I do not subscribe to the idea that taking money from wealthy people and giving it to poor people will fairly balance the equation.

I believe that education and training are two key resources needed by people living in poverty, and technology should make this more possible today than ever before. When we make educational and training opportunities available and accessible for everyone, and link the curricula to existing economic opportunities, we can make significant progress in helping people improve their lives and increase their incomes.

Prayer

God, help me to continue improving my skills and increasing my abilities.

Decision

Today I have decided to: _____

_____

_____

_____

_____

RETURNING CITIZENS

Verse

"Day by day the king gave Jehoiachin a regular allowance as long as he lived." 2 Kings 25:30

Thought

I recently received a letter from a young man who had spent a few years in prison for crimes he had committed. While he was incarcerated, he made many decisions about his life and how he planned to live after he was released. He had been released on parole and was very proud of his personal accomplishments since his release.

He had gotten employment that he described as a "good job." I smiled when I read that because I am old enough to remember when any job attained was a good job. Despite the difficulty that formerly incarcerated people have with securing housing, this young man had found a landlord who was willing to rent him an apartment – that was a huge victory. Finding housing can be more difficult than finding employment for people returning from penal institutions.

He had a few more achievements that he shared, and then went on to explain why he had decided to write to me. What he had not been able to accomplish was getting a new driver's license. His license had expired while he was in prison, and now he could not produce the many documents required by the motor vehicle agency in his state to qualify for a new driver's license. That one challenge, if not resolved, could have the impact of undermining all of the other progress that he had made.

There was no public transportation available as an option for commuting to his good job. Using Uber or Lyft was an unreliable and expensive solution. If he could not get to work, he would lose his job, and if he lost his job, he could not pay his rent and would lose his apartment, rendering him homeless. And so on. In short, he needed a driver's license.

While I was honored that he wrote to me, I was also very concerned. There are a few people that specialize in helping formerly incarcerated persons – returning citizens – as they transition back into their communities and society in general, and I am not one of them. Of course, I would connect him to an organization that specializes in that work, but it reminded me that more of us – including me – should be doing more of such work.

Jehoiachin, king of Judah, had been in prison for thirty-seven years when King Awel-Marduk of Babylon took personal responsibility to release him and help him transition back into his society. He even gave him an allowance for the rest of his life.

Awel-Marduk didn't have to do this, but I am sure Jehoiachin was grateful that he did and his life was changed forever.

Prayer

God, help me to be more useful to returning citizens and those that serve them in my community.

Decision

Today I have decided to: _____

_____

_____

_____

_____

HEALING SALT

Verse

*The people of the city said to Elisha, "Look, our
lord, this town is well situated, as you can see, but
the water is bad and the land is unproductive."
"Bring me a new bowl," he said, "and put salt in it."
So, they brought it to him. Then he went out to
the spring and threw the salt into it, saying, "This
is what the Lord says: 'I have healed this water.
Never again will it cause death or make the land
unproductive'".* 2 Kings 2:19-21 NIV

Thought

One of the characteristics that I love the most about the Bible
is that its stories align so beautifully with our reality wherever
we are and whenever we read it. My father was a minister, and
I could not understand how he could have something different
to say to the same people week after week. I often asked him
how he got his sermon topics, and he would always say they
came from the Bible.

Later in life, I understood what he meant. As opposed to
making a conclusion and then finding a Bible verse to affirm it

(isogesis), the better way is to allow a biblical text to reveal a truth to you after careful and thorough study (exegesis). Then the application of a text becomes natural and impactful.

This story illustrates my point so well. When we look at everything God made at creation, it seems that all creatures, parts of nature, and planets have functioned exactly as God intended when God made them. That is, everything except humans. God created humans to reflect God's character and God's nature; God created humans in the image of God.

But humans have opted to live in a manner that continuously rebels against God's original intent and purpose. Thus, we have wars, pollution, injustice, hatred, oppression, and all other ungodly characteristics that permeate our societies. Humanity has become a larger metaphor for what Elisha found in this city.

Everything in the city was fine, well-situated. Just one aspect of the city was bad and unproductive – the water. Bad water produces bad results in every other aspect of life. Just as bad people produce bad results in every aspect of life for humans. Elisha's solution was to have a bowl filled with salt and then to pour the salt into the water. The water was healed and the city was saved.

Jesus said that his disciples would be the salt of the earth. So, if the bowl in the Elisha's hand represents the church in the hands of God, then just as Elisha poured his salt into the water to heal it, so God pours salt (his disciples) from His bowl (the church) into bad waters (the world) to bring healing.

When Christians function as healers, we have the power to be salt in every area of human need. To that end, we should not simply seek financial health for ourselves, but we must become the salt that helps others achieve their financial healing.

Prayer

God, help me to become salt and to maintain my saltiness to aid someone's financial healing.

Decision

Today I have decided to: _____

_____

_____

_____

_____

DANGEROUS ILLUSIONS

Verse

"When they got up early in the morning, the sun was shining on the water. To the Moabites across the way, the water looked red – like blood. 'That's blood!', they said. Those kings must have fought and slaughtered each other. Now to the plunder, Moab." 2 Kings 3:22-23.

Thought

There are very creative people who deceive others into believing that they can achieve something great with little to no effort. In some instances, however, people are the victims of their own imaginations and fall prey to the schemes of their own dreams. It seems this was the case for the unfortunate Moabite soldiers who were convinced that their three enemies had killed each other and that a body of water was a pool of their blood.

We have no way of knowing or understanding exactly what happened, but it didn't take much for the Moabite army to convince itself that the kings of Israel, Judah and Edom had turned on each other and made it possible for them to finish them off effortlessly. Of course, we read later in this chapter that the Moabites were soundly defeated, and their towns and lands plundered.

What a bizarre and tragic occurrence in the life of a people! And what a warning for those who are convinced that get rich quick schemes and shortcuts to success are real.

Granted there is that handful of individuals who win multi-million-dollar lotteries, athletes awarded multi-million-dollar contracts to play a sport or single business transactions that yield exorbitant amounts of money. I have a friend who joined a company as a director, attended his first meeting where the board voted to sell the company, and he made one million dollars just by attending that one meeting.

However, none of these examples are normal and should not create any expectations in anyone's mind to alter their plans to work towards their goals. The tragedy was not that the water looked like blood to the Moabites or the thought that their enemies had destroyed themselves. The great tragedy was that they *changed* their plans and their strategy in response to those false assumptions.

I use the word 'tragic' because these people died as a result of their decision. There are those whose relationships, businesses and finances literally die when they make decisions based on erroneous information or wild assumptions.

I accept the adage, *"If something seems too good to be true, it probably is."*

Prayer

God, please protect me from those things that look too good to be true."

Decision

Today I have decided to: _____

_____

_____

_____

_____

www.dbsoaries.com

ALSO BY
DEFOREST B. SOARIES, JR.

Meditations for Financial Freedom Vol 1

Meditations for Financial Freedom Vol 2

Meditations for Financial Freedom Vol 3

Say Yes to No Debt: 12 Steps to Financial Freedom

dfree® Lifestyle: Say Yes to No Debt (Workbook)

Say Yes When Life Says No

Say Yes When Life Says No Workbook

Your dfree® for Seasoned Citizens:
A Resource for Senior Citizens

Your dfree® for Entrepreneurs:
A Resource for Entrepreneurs and the Self Employed

Your dfree® for Young Adults

ABOUT THE AUTHOR

DeForest B. Soaries, Jr., D.Min.

Dr. Soaries is the President and CEO of Corporate Community Connections, Inc., a company that assists corporations expand and improve their Corporate Social Responsibility efforts. In July 2021 he retired from 30 years of ministry as the third Senior Pastor of First Baptist Church of Lincoln Gardens ("FBCLG") in Somerset, New Jersey. His pastoral ministry focused on spiritual growth, educational excellence, economic empowerment, and faith-based community development. As a pioneer of faith-based community development, Dr. Soaries' impact on FBCLG and the community was tremendous. In 1992, he founded the Central Jersey Community Development Corporation ("CJCDC"), a 501(c)(3) non-profit organization that specializes in helping revitalize underserved and vulnerable neighborhoods. In 1996, the CJCDC launched Harvest of Hope Family Services Network, Inc. This organization developed permanent solutions for hundreds of foster children and parents.

Dr. Soaries was inducted to the The Martin Luther King Jr Board of Preachers at Morehouse College.

From 1999 to 2002, Dr. Soaries served as New Jersey's Secretary of State, making him the first and only African-

American male to serve in that office. He also served as the former chairman of the United States Election Assistance Commission, which was established by Congress to implement the "Help America Vote Act" of 2002.

In 2005, Dr. Soaries launched the dfree® Financial Freedom Movement. The dfree® strategy teaches people how to become financially self-sufficient. His work in financial empowerment was featured in a CNN documentary.

Dr. Soaries has written 10 books including "Say Yes to No Debt" and "Say Yes When Life Says No." he is the host of a weekly radio show "For Your Soul" on SiriusXM Urban View.

Dr. Soaries currently serves as an Independent Director at Independence Realty Trust, Ocwen Financial Corporation and the Federal Home Loan Bank of New York. He also serves as a Trustee of RWJ Barnabas Health.

Soaries earned a Bachelor of Arts Degree from Fordham University, a Master of Divinity Degree from Princeton Theological Seminary, and a Doctor of Ministry Degree from United Theological Seminary. Dr. Soaries resides in Monmouth Junction, New Jersey with his wife, Donna, and twin sons.

Made in the USA
Middletown, DE
01 February 2024

48900295R00057